Xmas 2007

To: Natalie

From: Dad

I love you always

Published by C.R. Gibson® Norwalk, CT 06856
C.R. Gibson® is a registered trademark of Thomas Nelson, Inc.
Made in the U.S.A.
ISBN 0-7667-3388-2
GB651

A Christmas Wish For You

Photographs by

Kim Anderson

Text by Julie Mitchell Marra

The C.R. Gibson® Company Norwalk, Connecticut

$\mathcal{A}$t Christmastime,
as the joy and excitement
of the countdown begins…

$\mathcal{E}$njoy this special time.

Remember when you were a child...
stringing popcorn for the tree,
singing Christmas carols,
standing in the soft snow
under a black sky
glimmering with bright stars...

Enjoy the wonder of Christmas.

emember when the
winter wind would blow...
and you'd hurry inside
to reach the warm love of home...

may you feel that way again.

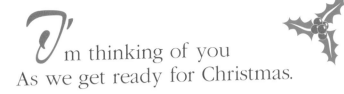

I'm thinking of you
As we get ready for Christmas.

I'm thinking of friends
coming to visit...

I'm thinking of families
getting together again...

I'm thinking of you.

$\mathcal{M}$ay you enjoy the
simple things…
decorating the house,
wrapping gifts
and baking cookies.

May you enjoy
the meaning of holiday...
singing hymns,
saying thanks
and feeling love.

As we send greetings
to friends both near and far...

remember, whether we're
together or apart
you share a special place
in my heart.

In the midst of the holiday rush,
shopping and wrapping
and sending gifts to everyone...

remember that the best gift
you can give is your love.

his year...

remember sledding and skating
and making the biggest snowman...

remember wishing and hoping
that Christmas would last forever!

The light of Christmas
is seen around the world.

The light of Christmas
warms every heart.

The light of Christmas
is shining for you.

*T*his Christmas
send glad tidings to neighbors,
teachers, family and friends.

Spread the joy of Christmas
to loved ones and strangers.

Help others to know that
no one is alone.

*T*ake time to smell
the scents of Christmas
and enjoy the candle glow.

*L*isten to the magical melody
 of Christmas.

Keep the enchantment in your heart
 all through the year.

As Christmas Eve
unfolds before you,
hold tight to the
wonder, mystery
and joy.

*M*ay Christmas renew
your childlike faith.

May Christmas fulfill
your hopes and prayers.

May Christmas
renew your spirit,
rekindle your hope
and make all of your
dreams come true.

Colophon:
Edited by Marilyn Moore
Designed by Jeanette Ulm

Type set in Charme,
Garamond Light and Garamond Bold